YES! WE ARE LATINOS

ALMA FLOR ADA and
F. ISABEL CAMPOY
PICTURES BY DAVID DIAZ

x

ini Charlesbridge

Published by Charlesbridge
85 Main Street
Watertown, MA 02472
(617) 926-0329
www.charlesbridge.com

Library of Congress Cataloging-in-Publication Data
Ada, Alma Flor.
    Yes! we are Latinos / Alma Flor Ada and F. Isabel Campoy; illustrated by David Diaz.
       p. cm.
    Text primarily in English; some words in Spanish.
    Includes bibliographical references and index.
    Summary: A collection of stories about young Latino immigrant experiences
in the United States.
    ISBN 978-1-58089-383-1 (reinforced for library use)
    ISBN 978-1-60734-618-0 (ebook)
1. Latin Americans—United States—Juvenile fiction. 2. Latin Americans—Cultural
assimilation—Juvenile fiction. 3. Immigrants—United States—Juvenile fiction.
4. Emigration and immigration—Fiction. [1. Latin Americans—United States—Fiction.
2. Immigrants—Fiction. 3. Emigration and immigration—Fiction. 4. Short stories.]
I. Campoy, F. Isabel. II. Diaz, David, ill. III. Title.
PZ7.A1857Yes 2013
[Fic]—dc23   2012027214

Printed in China
(hc) 10 9 8 7 6 5 4 3 2 1

Illustrations hand-cut from Rubylith, color work executed in Adobe Photoshop
Display type and text type set in *Periódico,* designed by Eduardo Manso
Printed and bound February 2013 by Jade Productions in Heyuan, Guangdong, China
Production supervision by Brian G. Walker
Designed by Susan Mallory Sherman

To all children
la esperanza del mundo
the hope of the world

And to the adults in their lives
who inspire them
to own their destiny
　　　　—A. F. A. & F. I. C.

To Miguel Angel Calderon
　　　　—D. D.

Contents

What Makes Someone Latino?

There are more than fifty million people in the United States who call themselves Latinos or Latinas—a population larger than that of many countries. Have you ever asked yourself what makes someone a Latino?

Latinos and Latinas come from diverse backgrounds. Some are descendants of the first Europeans who settled in what is today the United States: Spaniards who created cities like Saint Augustine, Florida; Santa Fe, New Mexico; El Paso, Texas; and Los Angeles, California. Many descend from families that lived in Texas, Arizona, and Colorado when the United States took those territories from Mexico as a war prize. Others immigrated to the United States at different times from Spanish-speaking countries.

Did you know that Latinos and Latinas live in every state? They do, in both urban and rural areas. Some Latinos are highly educated professionals, doctors, scientists, and artists. Some are entrepreneurs, starting and running their own businesses. Others work in farms or factories, doing hard manual labor.

Most Latinos and Latinas have mixed origins: they are mestizos, whether by blood or by culture. Their heritage includes roots from indigenous, African, and Spanish people, as well as the many others who have settled in Latin America over centuries.

This book offers only a sample of what Latinos and Latinas may look like. If you have Latino ancestry, it may raise questions about your own rich heritage. If you do not have Latino ancestry, we hope it will interest you to learn more about Latinas and Latinos. May you find wonderful friends among them!

Whatever your background, this book is an invitation to look inside yourself. What would your story tell us about you?

My Name Is Juanita

I am Mexican. I live in New York. I am Latina.

"Get up, Juanita—*levántate, m'hija.*"
My mother's voice is impatient.
"Come on, it's getting late.
I'll miss my bus."
I don't want to upset her, so I get up.
I sit at the table,
where breakfast is already waiting.
My brothers devour steaming tortillas and
huevos rancheros—
eggs cooked just as they like them.

We leave the apartment together.
"*¡Dios los bendiga, m'hijos!* May God bless you!"
my mother calls out,
rushing to catch the bus that will take her to work.
Between the tall buildings
of the never-ending street,

I can see a thin strip of sky.
On the sidewalk my feet crush dead leaves
that announce
soon the days will be cold.
My brothers' long legs
leave me behind.
Ramón and Ramiro will be at their middle school soon,
and I will still be crunching leaves
with my new sneakers.

I slow down even more, remembering how
different it was to go to school
at home, in Mexico,
walking on the narrow streets paved with stones,
among the round hills, always green.
We would gather as we walked—
Rosa, María, Elena, Lupe, and me—
without even realizing it,
like flowers
will sometimes bloom together in the same patch.
We arrived happily at our small school,
where time passed unnoticed.
We learned numbers and letters,
addition and subtraction.
But the best part of each day was our music.
We practiced our dances and songs
proudly, having been chosen
to perform them in the plaza.
I wish, though, that school had taught us
more about Mexico and my people.
Here the teacher talks
about the rich ancient civilizations
of the country of my birth,
and I know so little about it.

Finally the long sidewalk
splattered with brown leaves
brings me to the door of this new school
where my language, my sweet Mixtec,

is a secret language
that no one in this school
even suspects exists.
My teacher will greet me in Spanish:
"Buenos días, Juana."
I understand she believes
she is speaking my home language—
trying to make me feel good,
showing me that she has made the effort
to learn a little Spanish.
I smile at her, saying,
"Buenos días, Mrs. Johnston."
She reminds me of Sra. Sánchez,
my first teacher in Mexico,
who on the first day asked me
if I spoke Spanish.
When I said "No," she answered,
"You'll learn. Here we speak only Spanish."
Now, as then, I will struggle through the day
while the teacher speaks her own language—
this new language
with all those *w*'s.

Only today,
a surprise awaits me at school.
Next to the teacher stands a girl—
her skin the same rich color as mine,
her hair, black, long, and as straight as mine, and
her face showing the same surprise as mine—

a surprise that makes her dark eyes sparkle
like black obsidian in the sun.
Against the echo of cars and motorcycles
on the busy street outside, we cry out:
"¡Elena!"
"¡Juanita!"
Mrs. Johnston looks at us with surprise.
"Do you know each other?"
We smile in silence.
No explanations
to break the magic of the moment.
We have learned to smile
when we understand that silence is better
or when we don't understand.
We answer *"¡Sí!"* very softly
and keep our secret,
saving the rejoicing for later.

Recess will come, sometime,
and then we will be able to use our language—
our sweet Mixtec—
to share everything that has happened
since we said good-bye in our town,
the town that wakes up every morning
with the song of the roosters
and the cooing of doves.
But that will happen later.
Now smiling to each other is enough.

Our Indigenous Roots

Extraordinary civilizations developed in Mexico, Central America, and the Andean area of South America long before Europeans knew these places existed. The cities of Tenochtitlán (present-day Mexico City) and Cuzco (in present-day Peru), the magnificent pyramids built by the Mayas, and the fortresses of Sacsayhuaman in the Andes demonstrate the richness of these indigenous, or native, civilizations. These self-sustaining and highly developed societies had achieved impressive knowledge of mathematics and astronomy, and had created unique architectural wonders and original art: stone sculpture, clay pottery, exquisite weavings, and beautiful gold and turquoise jewelry. Some of their architectural and artistic creations remain unsurpassed today.

After Christopher Columbus sailed to the Caribbean in 1492, many European countries sought to colonize these lands. England and France occupied and colonized lands in the north: present-day Canada and the northern United States. Spain colonized present-day Texas, New Mexico, Arizona, California, Louisiana, and Florida, as well as Mexico, the major Caribbean islands, and most of Central and South America. Other areas in Central and South America were colonized by France, the Netherlands, Denmark, and Portugal. The Caribbean islands were particularly attractive to Europeans because their climate was ideal for growing sugarcane and spices.

The original population of the islands disappeared almost

entirely. Some indigenous people were wiped out by illness brought involuntarily by the Europeans. Others died as a result of forced hard labor. Some committed suicide because they would not bear being held in servitude. A large number of people were forcefully brought from Africa.

The European colonizers thought that new civilizations could rise only on the ashes of the conquered nations. To impose their civilization and their religion, which they considered superior, the Spaniards destroyed most of what they encountered. Fortunately they also wrote chronicles about what they saw and encouraged mestizos, such as Garcilaso de la Vega and Huamán Poma de Ayala in Peru, to write what they knew about the culture of their ancestors. Much of what we know today about those extraordinary civilizations comes from the work of archaeologists, but also from chronicles written at the time of the conquest and colonization.

After more than three hundred years of being ruled by

Spain, the people in the Spanish colonies began to rebel and demand their rights as independent nations. Some also wanted to abolish slavery. Over much of the nineteenth century, all the Spanish colonies except Puerto Rico gained their independence and abolished slavery.

While these countries have Spanish as their primary language, many other languages are also spoken there. The indigenous cultures of the Americas had their own languages. Tragically, some of these languages disappeared, as native speakers died or were killed. But some languages have survived, including Nahuatl, Maya, Zapotec, and Mixtec in Mexico; Quiché in Guatemala; and Quechua and Aymara in Peru and Bolivia.

Language is one of the most important elements of any culture. When the language is alive, the culture is alive, too. But even though indigenous languages and cultures have disappeared or been diminished, the majority of Latin American inhabitants have indigenous roots. As the poet José Martí once wrote, the children of the Americas should learn to know, respect, and love the indigenous mother of this continent.

My Name Is Mónica

I am from El Salvador. I live in Houston.
I am Texan. I am Latina.

Mom's eyes were so swollen, her face so red,
when I got home from school.
I could see she had been crying for hours.
This was five years ago, in El Salvador.
All she could say was,
"Your father went to the North."
We waited anxiously for weeks for his first letter.
From then on, always the same message:
"Soon you'll be here with me."
It was three years before I saw him again.
We moved to Mexico to be closer to the North,
staying with my aunt, Tía Vicky,
who had been living there for many years,
cleaning and cooking for Mrs. Randall,
a lady on the other side, in Laredo, Texas.
coming home only on Sundays.

Tía Vicky could go back and forth
across the border with no trouble.
Years ago she married a young Texan,
so she became an American citizen, too.
But he was in the military
and died shortly after they were married.
Now he smiles forever, dressed in his uniform,
in the large photo with the silver frame
hanging on the wall.

One day Mrs. Randall and her niece
came to our house.
My aunt told me I would be going with them.
"But first," she said, "we must cut your hair."
I started crying for my braids.
My braids went everywhere with me.

I was used to feeling their weight on my back.
They bounced as I walked
and patted me as I ran.
"I'll save your braids for you," Tía Vicky assured me.
I still have them, wrapped in tissue paper.
Then she put a barrette with pink flowers
on my short hair.
Mrs. Randall gave me a dress from her niece
and took me to get a pair of new shoes.
When we got to the border, she said,
"My nieces,"
and the border patrol guard
just waved his hand
and let us pass.

I lived several months with kind Mrs. Randall
without seeing my mother.
Every week my aunt brought a letter
from Mom, promising we would soon be together.
Every week my father called on the phone
and told me the same thing.
But it never happened.
Then one afternoon,
when I came home from school,
there was a woman in the living room,
standing there, waiting.
At first I didn't recognize her.
They had colored her hair
just like my aunt's,

made up her face
just like my aunt's.
She was wearing
one of my aunt's dresses.
She looked so like my aunt—
so different from Mom—
that it took me a moment
to rush into her arms.
"They finally decided I could come across
with Tía Vicky's passport.
Mrs. Randall will take it back to her
in a few weeks."
For a while we stayed
at Mrs. Randall's,
with Mom doing the work my aunt used to do,
waiting to agree with my father on what we should do.

Now we live in Houston.
Dad has been working here for a while.
He has done many odd jobs,
but now he is the janitor
in a building
with many law offices.
And one of the lawyers
is helping,
trying to get us papers,
legal papers,
so we won't be illegal

anymore,
so I won't have to be
afraid
of the Migra—
having nightmares
that they send back my parents
and I stay
all alone
in this big city.

My father says *illegal*
is a dirty word.
All human beings
are made legal
by God
when they are born.
"Say *undocumented*,"
he insists,
"if you need to call it something."
Illegal or undocumented—
I do not care.
I am glad I won't have to be
any of that anymore
and just be me—
Mónica,
daughter, niece, friend,
student,
girl.

Latino Immigration to the United States

The history of humankind is a history of migrations. All through history people have moved from one area to another in search of better living conditions. Sometimes they have moved peacefully into vacant lands. Many times their migrations have been forceful, by moving into and conquering lands previously claimed by others. But how rightful were those claims?

The United States was built by immigrants. Except for those with full Native American heritage, everyone living here has ancestors from another part of the world. Some people have remained attached to their cultural heritage and can trace where their ancestors came from. Others, due to geographic moves, intermarriage, or other reasons, cannot really tell where their ancestors originated.

Spanish speakers were established in the United States before English speakers. Some Latinos today are descendants of those first Spanish-speaking settlers; others immigrated later. Latinos continue to immigrate to the United States in significant numbers, in many ways and for many reasons.

Some Latinos come to study. They intend to return to their countries, but while in the United States they receive a job offer, get married, or simply decide to stay.

Some Latinos come for what they think will be a short visit to relatives or friends. Once in the United States, they like

the idea of spending a longer time. They may eventually get a job or buy a house, and leaving becomes a distant thought.

Some Latinos have come because of political unrest in their home countries—war, dictatorships, or insecurity. Since the United States often has influence on the events in their countries, they find it appropriate to seek asylum here.

Just like previous immigrants to this country—British, Scottish, Irish, German, Italian, Polish, Russian, Swedish, Danish, as well as Jewish people of many nationalities—the majority of Latinos come in search of better living conditions.

The reasons for global poverty, both for individuals and for countries, are complex and must be addressed. But all people need to have enough to feed and clothe their children, to keep them safe and healthy, and to give them an education that will lead to opportunity. The United States became a great nation through the work of immigrants from many parts of the world. Today there is still much work to be done. New immigrants want to do that work, just as the immigrants of the past have done.

Crossing the border without papers or with false papers is breaking the law. But not all laws are just, moral, or ethical. The law that allowed people to be held as slaves was wrong. The laws that prohibited enslaved people of African descent to learn to read was wrong. The law that prohibited women to vote was wrong. The law that segregated blacks from whites in the southern states, so that African American children could not go to the same schools as white children, was wrong.

The United States has one hundred senators, four hundred thirty-five representatives, and fifty state governments to enforce, debate, amend, and repeal our laws. When laws are insufficient or unjust, due to new realities or new understandings, we look to our lawmakers and fellow citizens to change those laws for the better. Today we recognize as heroes people such as Rosa Parks, Martin Luther King, Jr., César Chávez, and Fred Korematsu, who challenged unjust laws of the past.

Immigration is one of the most important issues in the United States. Our country could not function without the work of immigrants. How many immigrants can the country admit? How can we ensure that those who come into the country will obey the laws and become productive citizens?

Many people are debating these issues. In the meantime, thousands of immigrant families continue to live, work, and study as they seek a better life.

My name Is José Miguel—not Joe, not Mike

I am Cuban and Nicaraguan. I live in Tampa, Florida. I am Latino.

"*Adiós*, José Miguel.
Have a good day, *hijo.*
Aprende mucho—learn all you can."
Just as he does every day,
my grandfather comes to the door
to say good-bye to me,
giving me advice as I leave for school.
He says he wishes he had been able
to do that for his own son, my father.
The sky is covered with dark clouds,
so I rush.
School is not far,
but the rain could begin any minute.
Here in Florida the sky
goes from blue to black in an instant

and you get soaked
before you even realize it is raining.
Roger catches up with me
before the rain does.
I would have rather gotten soaked.
He slaps me on the back,
pretending to be friendly
but making sure it hurts.
"Made many tacos, today,
  Miguuuel?" he asks.

"What are you using
  in them now? Dog meat?"
  He laughs and lets go of me
  because we are already at school,
  and Mr. Tate is standing
  in the yard
  watching us.
  Ever since
  Miguel's Tacos
  opened a couple of blocks
  away from school,
  the kids have been teasing me.
  Before it used to be all about
"No way, José,"
  and now
  it's all about Miguel's Tacos.
"It would be easier,"
  Mr. Tate keeps saying to me,
"if you would let us call you
  Joe or Mike.
  It would let you blend in."
  Yesterday I got tired
  of his words.
"Do you know who
  Cervantes is, Mr. Tate?"
  I asked him politely.
"Don Miguel de Cervantes?
  Or Miguel de Unamuno,
  or Miguel Hernández?

Look them up, Mr. Tate."
I was very sure to keep
my tone soft, my words polite.
"Google them.
Then you would know
why I can't be called Mike."
I think I impressed him.
I doubt he will come back
with that Mike business again.
Although the truth is that
I wasn't named
for Miguel de Unamuno,
or Miguel Hernández,
or Cervantes.
I was named
after my grandfather,
José Miguel Martínez,
who never wrote a word
but every morning
walks out to the door
to say good-bye
and tell me to learn much.
That is why I will not be Joe,
or Mike,
in spite of all the Rogers in the world,
but José Miguel Martínez.
Cubano, a mucha honra. Yes, very proud
to be Cuban.
Para servirle. And at your service.

Cuba and the United States

Cubans have been a part of the United States for a very long time. The first European explorers and settlers in Florida were Spaniards departing from Cuba under the leadership of Ponce de León. The cities of Saint Augustine, Tampa, Ybor City, and Key West (Cayo Hueso) were all founded by people coming from Cuba, and through the years many Cubans moved to these cities.

While all the continental Spanish colonies had achieved their independence by the mid-nineteenth century, Cuba and Puerto Rico had not. As the last Spanish colonies in the Americas—the "last jewels of the Spanish crown"—the Spaniards held on to them with concentrated efforts, and it had been hard for the island citizens to acquire weapons to defend themselves. Cuban and Puerto Rican patriots created the Revolutionary Party, with offices in New York under the leadership of the poet and visionary José Martí. The intent was to liberate both islands: first Cuba, then Puerto Rico.

Cuba's first war to gain its independence lasted from 1868 to 1878. After heavy losses on both sides, a truce was signed. The second major war started in 1895. There was no doubt this time that Cuba would win.

The United States had recently acquired California, extending its boundaries all the way to the Pacific. Now it was looking for islands to control. The US colonized Hawaii easily, after American missionaries purchased large tracts of land and destroyed the indigenous identity by promoting a new

religion and language. The United States Congress supported the "Manifest Destiny" doctrine, asserting that the islands neighboring the United States were destined to become part of the nation. Cuba became, in the words of one congressman, "the ripe apple about to fall from the tree."

In 1898 the United States declared war on Spain, fighting in Cuba and in the Philippines, one of Spain's Pacific colonies. Spain, debilitated from years of fighting to preserve its colonies, had neither the strength nor the willingness to fight the United States. The war the Cubans had been winning suddenly became a United States victory instead.

For the Cubans it was a profound shock. They had fought long and hard against one master and certainly did not want to end up with another. The United States occupied Cuba from 1898 to 1902, as US companies secured large fields of sugarcane, railroads, and electricity and other utilities. When the United States turned over the government to the Cubans on May 20, 1902, there were still important US economic interests on the island. To preserve them, the United States added an amendment to the Cuban constitution reserving the right to approve the results of Cuban presidential elections. All of this would sour further Cuban relations with the United States.

During the 1950s Cuba was ruled by Fulgencio Batista, a repressive dictator. Cuban society was sharply divided by class and income: a small but powerful upper class, a successful middle class, and a majority of the population living in great poverty. A group of young Cubans, led by Fidel Castro and Che Guevara, initiated a revolution to depose Batista. They installed a new government intending to offer jobs, medical care, and education to the whole population.

The Cuban upper class, many of whom were fluent in English and had business connections in the United States, left the island quickly, closely followed by other professionals and business people. This first group of Cuban immigrants, mostly white and highly educated, soon became successful in the United States.

The new Cuban government appropriated businesses that had belonged to American corporations. The United States, in the middle of the Cold War against communism, feared that Cuba's revolutionary party posed a national threat and initiated a blockade that made it impossible for Cuba to obtain oil and other necessary products from the United States or Latin America. The Soviet Union saw the possibility of having an ally in the American continent and offered Cuba oil support. Over the years, while the Cuban Revolution made great progress in medicine and education, the island's economic situation declined, deteriorating further with the dissolution of the Soviet Union.

Many Cubans have left Cuba in search of better economic opportunities. In 1980 Cubans living in the United States were granted permission to travel by boat from Florida, only seventy miles away, to the port of Mariel in Cuba to bring back their relatives and friends. They were also forced to bring back with them other Cubans who wanted to leave the island. As many as 125,000 Cubans came to the United States as part of the Mariel Boat Lift.

Cubans coming to the United States are considered political exiles: if they succeed in stepping on American soil, they are immediately granted documentation to become legal residents. The present-day immigration of Cubans has transformed the city of Miami from a small, quaint vacation town into a vibrant, dynamic city known as a Latin American capital of finance and entertainment.

While not as numerous as other Latino groups, Cubans are highly educated, which has helped them achieve significant professional, artistic, and entrepreneurial success.

My Name Is Gladys

I am Puerto Rican.
I live in Philadelphia.
I am Latina.

My mother is so busy with my sister's *quinces*.
She keeps calling on me to help.
"Gladys, *ven hijita, por favor*."
Yolanda's *quinceañera* party
is all we have been talking about
in my family
for the longest time.
It's all about
the dress,
the tiara,
the cake,
the music,
the court of fourteen boys and girls
that will accompany her
in her rite of passage,
when all of a sudden
everyone will agree

she is no longer a girl
but a full-grown woman.

I love parties
with good music—
dancing lets me feel so free—
and there's no question
Yolanda will be lovely
in her full, long dress.
"Just like a princess,"
they all said when she tried it on.
Mom, Abuelita, *las tías y las primas,*

everyone was repeating,
"Como una princesa."
I will not say anything
until the party is over.
I plan to dance
all night long.
But when Mami
begins to talk
about *mis quinces*—
and I'm sure
she will begin soon—
I'll tell her
the family does not need
to go broke again.
I love to dance,
but I don't need
an elaborate party—
a *quinceañera* production—
to know I'm becoming a woman.
I just don't believe it happens
in one day—
and what I want is something else.

I want Dad to stop saying
that it's not a good idea
to go to college.
"Why all that study, *m'hijita*?
Why go through all that?

You need to learn to be a good wife,
hijita, a good mother, and that's that."
I don't know if I will be a wife.
That requires finding someone, someday.
And if I become a mother,
I would try to be
as good as mine.
But before that
I need to become all I can be.
I want to go to college
and study.
I know it costs a lot,
and I'm not asking for the money.
I only ask that you not discourage me,
not make things any harder for me.
I will apply for work-study, loans, and scholarships,
like the counselor explained.
She insisted that
I must get very good grades
in junior high, so I will be well prepared for high school.
Encouragement to go on,
to succeed, to do better than my parents,
as they did better than theirs.
Going to college is my dream.
I want my parents
to encourage me.
That's the *quinces* gift
that I want.

The Pride of Being *Boricua*

The Spanish-American War also affected Puerto Rico. The United States demanded as war prizes the last of Spain's colonies: the Philippines, Guam, and the Mariana Islands in the Pacific; and Puerto Rico and the Virgin Islands in the Caribbean.

Puerto Rico became part of the US Commonwealth, which also includes Guam and the Mariana Islands. The United States owns Puerto Rico, but it is not a state. Puerto Ricans are citizens of the United States, but they cannot vote in presidential elections.

Some Puerto Ricans believe the island should become independent, since it has all the elements that usually define a nation: its own territory, language, culture, history, and traditions. Others prefer the status quo, noting that if Puerto Rico were an independent nation, Puerto Ricans would no longer be US citizens. A third group feels that, after so many years of association with the United States, Puerto Rico should become a state, with the same rights as Hawaii and all other states.

As US citizens, Puerto Ricans can immigrate to the United States fairly easily in search of economic opportunities. Many speak Spanish, especially more recent arrivals. Some older immigrants chose not to teach Spanish to their children, thinking it would help them assimilate more easily if they spoke only English. But many of these second-generation

Puerto Ricans now find it hard to travel to their parents' homeland and communicate with their relatives.

In spite of its small size, Puerto Rico is a nation of great energy and cultural richness. Music, literature, and art flourish on the island. Writers such as Esmeralda Santiago, Pura Belpré, and Nicholasa Mohr have enriched literature both in English and Spanish. Other well-known Puerto Rican artists include painter Antonio Martorell, actress Rita Moreno, and drummer Tito Puente.

Puerto Ricans have also made important contributions to the US workforce. Puerto Ricans can be found in every state and industry, though most have settled in cities along the East Coast and in the Midwest. Besides contributing their manual and professional work, Puerto Ricans are often politically active, and many have become educators, including Antonia Pantoja, Ricardo Fernández, Tony Baez, María Torres-Guzmán, and Carlota del Portillo.

My Name Is Santiago

I am Dominican.
I live in Detroit.
I am Latino.

After yesterday's game
my body aches,
all of it.
"Playing is important,"
my father says with pride
whenever we win a baseball game.
"But studying is more important,"
he will immediately add.
"You don't want to break your back
every day, like I do.
You want to use your head,
tener un trabajo decente,
have a decent job, my son."
And he goes on to tell me
how many great things
I can do in life.
He thinks I do not listen,

because I keep to myself.
I know who Trujillo was,
the horrors that took place
and all the misery
Abuelo went through
in that island they
call La República—
a place where they suffered so much
but can't forget.
I haven't told him yet.
I do have a secret dream.
Here under the shower,
as I let the hot water soften up my muscles,

I can even say it out loud,
"Yes! I will! Yes! I will!"
I will become a doctor.
I will go back to the island,
where many young children
die
because there is no care
for them.
I will create a hospital.
"Yes! I will!"
But for now
it will be my secret.
I do not want
Pedro and Domingo
to laugh at me.
Pedro already dropped out
of high school.
Domingo says he can't wait
to be out of school.
That's why my father
keeps repeating to me:
studying is important.
And I know.
And I will.
¡Sí, lo haré!
Yes! I will! For all of us.

From an Island to a Continent

The Dominican Republic occupies half of the Caribbean island of Hispaniola. The other half is the republic of Haiti. The Dominican Republic suffered through the long and cruel dictatorship of Rafael Trujillo, known as El Jefe, or "the chief," from 1930 to 1961. A few people close to Trujillo became very wealthy, while the country as a whole became impoverished. Many people emigrated to the United States to survive.

Although the Dominican Republic is geographically small, it has been home to many notable people. Salomé Ureña was one of the first women writers in Latin America. Her son Pedro Henríquez Ureña was a scholar and the Charles Eliot Norton Professor of Poetry at Harvard University for 1940–1941.

Two important contemporary Latin American authors are Latinos of Dominican origin. The novelist Junot Díaz won the Pulitzer Prize for fiction in 2008. Julia Alvarez writes for readers of all ages: her novel *How the García Girls Lost Their Accents* is based on her own family's experiences fleeing the Trujillo regime.

Dominicans have excelled in many areas. The Dominican Oscar de la Renta is one of the world's best known fashion designers. The Dominican Republic is also the birthplace of dozens of Major League Baseball players, including David Ortiz, Albert Pujols, Manny Ramirez, Alfonso Soriano, and Vladimir Guerrero.

My Name Is *Sultana, o Susana*

I am Sephardic.
I live in San Francisco.
I am Latina.

"Susana, Sultanica, breakfast is ready."
    My grandmother's voice
is as soft and caressing as her hands.
"Your mother isn't up yet.
She came home very late from the hospital.
But you should have your breakfast
and enjoy this glorious day."
    The table seems set up for a banquet,
with a grand centerpiece.
They are only flowers from our garden,
greens that some people would call weeds,
but Abuelita has arranged them
as if they were a bouquet from a flower shop.

The orange juice, molten gold in a glass, is fresh.
The milk is cold, just as I like it.
The butter melts on the warm bread.
Now I'll have to choose among the jams,
their bright colors shining like jewels in the glass jars.
    I eat slowly,
enjoying the food and the simple flowers
so carefully arranged,
listening to Abuelita repeat the words I hear every day.

"What a privilege you have being able to go to school.
What a pleasure to be able to study.
What a joy to be able to become whatever
you want to be—
a nurse like your mother, or a doctor,
a writer like your grandfather,
a dentist like your uncle,
or anything, whatever it may be,
you want to be . . ."

Her voice, which started so strong, so assertive,
becomes so soft I can hardly hear her:
"Sometimes, when I am here,
in the kitchen,
fixing dinner,
or while I weed the yard,
I think of all the things you could grow up to be."
I smile at her,
still savoring the orange jam on my bread,
and say:
"Abu, I don't know what I want to be."
Her eyes are fixed on mine.
I wait a minute, then add:
"But I do know *how* I want to be.
I want to be just like you!"
She smiles.
I get up, saying,
"I'll do the dishes. When I finish,
would you teach me the song you sang me yesterday?"

And we sit on the plastic chairs
in our small backyard,
under the shade
of the next-door neighbor's tree.
Abuelita begins the old song:
    "Tres hermanicas eran,
    blancas de rosa y ramas de flor,
    tres hermanicas eran,
    tres hermanicas son."
    There were three young sisters,
    white as roses, flowering branches.
    They were three young sisters,
    three young sisters they are.
In the middle of the song,
she stops and looks up at the sky.
"There must always have been clouds,"
she says.
"Maybe there were clouds,
just like these,
so white, so light, so innocent,
as they were leaving their homes. . . ."
She continues singing:
    "En medio del camino,
    blancas de rosa y ramas de flor
    en medio del camino
    castillos la fraguó."
    In the middle of the road,
    white as roses, flowering branches,

in the middle of the road,
castles he built for her.
"This song is more than five hundred years old.
We lived then in Spain.
And because of fear,
of mistrust,
we had to flee,
leaving everything behind.
But we took with us the language
and the songs,
and we have lived with them,
in them,
wherever we have been."
        No matter how many times
Abu has told me these stories,
I want to hear them again.
        Because of what she has told me,
I knew how to respond when my teacher,
wanting to make me feel proud,
said,
"It's wonderful that you are bilingual."
I explained,
"I am trilingual. I speak English
and Spanish,
but my first language is Ladino,
the Sephardic language."
Abuelita continues singing,
and I sing along.

Ladino Language and the Cultural Identity of Sephardic Jews

In the year 711 a group of Arab warriors invaded the Iberian Peninsula (present-day Spain and Portugal) and took control of most of its land. Over the next eight hundred years, small Christian kingdoms developed in the northern part of the peninsula and slowly began to reconquer territories from the Arabs.

Periods of peace and war alternated, and diverse alliances were formed. But more and more the Christian kingdoms became united, by conquest, treaties, or marriages, and managed to occupy cities previously developed and held by Muslim rulers. In the fifteenth century the marriage of Isabella of Castilla and Fernando of Aragón, known as *los Reyes Católicos,* or the Catholic Monarchs, united most of the peninsula under their rule. In 1492 they occupied the last remaining Muslim kingdom and took over the magnificent city of Granada, in Andalucía. The Muslim rulers of the city fled to nearby Morocco, seventy miles away on the northern coast of Africa—a desert region, very different from the rich farmland of Al-Andalus, or Andalucía.

For many centuries Jewish people had lived on the peninsula. After the Arab invasion, some Jews lived in Christian kingdoms, but many lived in Muslim cities. The Moors, or Muslim rulers, were not only tolerant of the Jewish people,

but also charged them lower taxes than the Christians did. After the conquest of Granada, the Catholic Monarchs were afraid that the Jews would aid the Moors in recapturing Granada. Ultimately they ordered all Jews remaining on the peninsula to convert to Catholicism or be expelled.

Some Jewish people were willing to convert: for them, religion was more a matter of tradition and culture than deep faith. Some of them and their descendants became so zealous in their new faith that they became Catholic priests and nuns. One of the greatest saints of the Catholic church, poet and mystic Santa Teresa of Ávila, was descended from converts.

For other Jews, the idea of leaving their homeland was too painful to endure, yet they were not willing to change their beliefs. They decided to keep their beliefs to themselves, though in public they accepted baptism and attended Catholic masses. In their hearts and in the privacy of their homes, they continued being true to their Jewish faith.

Those Jewish people who considered their religion central to their being refused to convert. They made the painful choice to leave their homeland, their homes, and all their possessions behind.

The expulsion of the Jews had terrible consequences for Spain. To determine whether their conversions were genuine, the Great Inquisitor Torquemada—descended from converts himself—led the Inquisition in Spain, committing great injustices and crimes against the Jews.

By expelling the Jews, Spain also lost some of its most creative and educated people. Spain once had great scientists, doctors, philosophers, and writers of Jewish ancestry; after 1492 they scattered through the world, in different areas of the Mediterranean and Europe.

The Jews who left Spain are known as Sephardic. They took with them memories of the land where they had lived for generations, the language they had spoken there, and the songs they had sung. Although Sephardic people settled in many places and learned the languages of their new countries, they maintained Ladino as the language of their home and prayers. Ladino incorporates some words from other languages, but it remains essentially the Spanish language of the fifteenth century, very close to the language Cervantes spoke. Today in Toledo, Spain, El Tránsito Synagogue and Sephardic Museum celebrates the richness of the Sephardic culture.

My Name Is Julio

I am Zapotec.
I live in Stockton, California.
I am Latino.

The truck zigzags as my father
avoids the holes
filled with last night's rain.
"I have to fix the suspension,"
he mumbles to himself,
knowing that it would take the savings
from a month's work
in the fields.
There is no sunshine yet.
My father has to be in the asparagus fields
before sunrise.
I catch a ride to school in his truck.
The truck is old and beat up,
but it's my father's pride.
Because he owns a truck,
he can sleep at home with us,
not in the barracks with the other men.
It's much better this way—
with what Dad had to pay the farmer

who owns the asparagus fields
to live and eat in the barracks,
he can pay the rent on our house.
Mom feeds all of us,
and we can be a family again.
My father is very skilled.
He knows exactly how to dig
and lift the asparagus stalks out of the ground
without breaking them.

He also knows how to plant them right—
deep enough but not too deep,
with the ground loose enough but not too loose—
so that the new asparagus will grow
to perfection.
Because he's such a good worker,
the owner has made him foreman
and sold him this old truck.
He could not have bought it at a dealer,
because he has no driver's license,
but he drives very carefully,
early in the morning and late at night.
We can live nearby
and see him every day.
Not like before,
when he was here and we were still there.

The most important thing,
he says,
is that we are learning many things,
my brother, Sergio, my sister, María, and I.
School is hard
because no one there knows our language,
Zapotec.
We are in bilingual classes,
where they teach us
using Spanish and English.
I don't understand much Spanish,
and English is still a mystery to me.

So many times
when the teacher talks and talks,
I keep my eyes open,
looking ahead
to the front of the class,
but what I'm seeing are the green fields
around our home,
our own town,
in Teotitlán del Valle.
There, we woke up every morning
to the sound of the looms.
Toc, toc, toc,
went the looms,
as the bright-colored threads
created the designs on the tapestries.
In our town we took the sheep
to graze on the hills,
and went hunting *chapulines*
that our mothers would fry with chile.
In our town there are doves,
white as the clouds or dark as the nights.
The cornstalks move with the breeze,
and the fields are covered with crawling
squash plants.
At shearing time
we helped bring the sheep in,
and my father would shear them, one by one,
taking their compact wool all in one piece.

It was as if he had undressed them
for the summer.
My mother would clean the wool first
with a steel brush,
taking away seeds, twigs, anything clinging to it.
Then the wool would be washed
in huge tubs of boiling water,
and then it would be brushed again
with a much finer brush.
A long process to turn
the wool into those colored threads
that make the designs
that live inside our hearts
for generations.
Those designs are still carved in the broken walls
of Monte Albán,
the magnificent city that was once
one of the most beautiful in the world.
"Julio," Ms. Grace repeats, "where are you?"
"In Monte Albán," I respond without thinking.
"Tell us about it," the teacher says. Then she adds,
"I was there once,
and your friends
should learn about its beauty."

Migrant Farmworkers

In the United States before the Industrial Revolution, farmers ate most of the food they raised. When they had surplus crops, they sold them at farmers' markets, where they bought other products. In some states, especially in the South, large landowners had other people work their land. Most were enslaved people of African descent, whose unjust treatment by their masters sparked the Civil War, to abolish slavery.

Like the factory model for manufactured goods, a large-scale model of agriculture developed over time. A few individuals or companies own large amounts of land, which they pay others to farm and manage. In some cases, the owner oversees the farm; in others, the owner leases the land to other people. Leased land can be leased again in smaller parcels, so some people can earn money without ever working the land. By the time all the owners and leaseholders have taken their cut of the farm's profits, there is almost nothing left for the workers who actually plant and harvest the crops.

Although much agricultural work has been mechanized, with tractors, plows, and specialized machines, much work still needs to be done by hand, particularly the picking and sorting of crops. Agricultural work is hard. Farmworkers spend many hours sweating in the sun, sometimes starting as early as five in the morning and working till ten at night. In addition to the risks from sun exposure, dust in the fields and chemical pesticides and fertilizers can also damage workers' health.

Some crops are grown and harvested year-round, but many are seasonal, and workers are needed only at certain times of the year for weeding, planting, pruning, or picking. Many workers follow the crops, picking strawberries in Southern California, then lettuce or artichokes in central California, then pears or walnuts farther north, and finally apples in Oregon and Washington. It is especially hard for migrant families, never having a stable home, living in run-down camps, and moving from school to school with new teachers and classmates every month or two.

Many workers in factories and other industries formed unions to fight for better working conditions, including a forty-hour work week, a day off every week, and health and disability insurance from their employers. But agricultural work is not protected by the laws that protect the rights of other workers. During the civil rights struggles in the 1960s and 1970s, farmworkers established the United Farm Workers (UFW), under the leadership of César Chávez. It managed to get some protection for some of the workers. But the largest numbers of growers do not comply with the requests of the UFW, and most workers are not protected by it.

Most people born and raised in the United States, unless they come from a farm tradition, would refuse to do agricultural work. A great deal of this work is done by people who come from Mexico, Central America, and the Caribbean. Because life is also very difficult in those countries, they are willing to sacrifice in order to help their families.

People work raising chickens, pigs, and cattle, and killing, cleaning, and processing the meat before it reaches our table. They plant the wheat that provides the flour for all the bread, crackers, cookies, and pastries we eat. They plant, tend, and gather the grains, the beans, the rice, the vegetables, the fruit. Every time we have a meal, we must remember that people have worked very hard so we can eat whatever we are eating.

My Name Is Felipe

**I am Panamanian and Venezuelan.
I am black. I live in Chicago.
I am Latino.**

***"Tus manos, hijo,* your hands."**
My mother's voice
is filled with sadness
and worry.
    "Don't be upset, Mami.
No es nada, you'll see—
it's nothing. I'll be all right."
I try to hide my hands,
damaged
from the fight.
    She continues,
"Those hands of yours
have much to do, much to paint. . . .
You have a gift, *hijo.*
Don't let anything harm your hands."
    I hug her tightly
and kiss her.
I hate to add to her worries.

She's got plenty already.
But I could not let those guys
get away with teasing Angelita.
    No one of us can decide
how we will be born.
Some are born
white, some black
like me,
some are born short, some tall
like me.

A person can work out
to get stronger,
and study
to get smarter.
But when someone is born
like Angelita,
that's just how she is.
    Tía Marcelina
works hard with her
every day,
helping her learn to help herself.
And she does improve
a little,
but she is how she is.
    Soft and loving,
that's Angelita,
kind and loving,
with her sweet smile.
    And if those guys
can't see it,
that's too bad.
But then they should go
on their way.
    I will not let them
tease her
or hurt her.
    "Be her champion,"
Mom told me.

And I'm trying to.
But I am not going to do it by fighting.
I won't damage my hands.
I'll be her champion in a different way.
    Last night,
when the pain in my hands kept me awake,
I saw it.
I will create paintings,
on huge canvases,
with colors no one has seen before.
Light will shine through them from behind.
I will call my paintings
the A Series.
People will wonder,
"Will there be a B Series? a C . . . ?"
I will only smile
and let them wonder.
Only I will know the answer:
A is for *Angelita*, like in the light
that shines through Angelita—
so easy to see
if you forget labels like
impaired, limited, and
Down syndrome,
and simply look
at her smile
and her shining eyes.

Deep African Roots

One of the most horrendous crimes ever committed by human beings has been to hold others in bondage or slavery.

People have been enslaved throughout human history, at different times and in different places. The United States, along with England, France, Portugal, and Spain, participated in transatlantic slave trading, capturing thousands of people in Africa and transporting them in inhuman conditions across the Atlantic Ocean to work as slaves on southern plantations.

African captives came from various lands and brought with them many cultural elements: different languages, among them Mandingo or Malinke, Congo, Calabari, and Lucumí; music, dance, songs, and musical instruments; religious beliefs and practices; and oral literature—myths, legends, stories, and poems. Along with their inner strength, creativity, and powerful appreciation of life, these cultural elements have become integral parts of the mestizo inheritance of Latin America.

The presence of people of African descent is more prevalent in the Caribbean islands and in the lowlands of South America, close to the coasts, where the large sugarcane plantations existed. But the African culture and worldview has been an important part of the cultural makeup of all Latin America.

The poet Nicolás Guillén is one of the most recognized Latin Americans of African descent. His powerful poems reflect the suffering of his people and also the pride he takes in

his heritage. In "El apellido" (The Last Name), he regrets the loss of the history of African people forced into slavery, and uses his lack of an African last name as a symbol of that loss. In "Balada de los dos abuelos" (Ballad of the Two Grandfathers), he recognizes his dual ancestry in the persons of two grandfathers: one the slave, the other the slave owner. At the end of the poem, after having denounced slavery and its injustice, he brings both grandfathers face-to-face to embrace each other, in an act of hope, in the blood running through his veins.

There have been Latin Americans of African descent in all aspects of life, from literature and music to politics, religion, and sports. Notable Latinos and Latinas with African heritage include the Mexican governor of California Pío de Jesús Pico, the saint San Martín de Porres, and the Cuban independence war leaders Antonio and José Maceo. Musicians such as Nicomedes Santa Cruz, Victoria Santa Cruz, and Susana Baca have restored Afro-Peruvian folklore. Singers Celia Cruz, Pablo Milanés, and Ibrahim Ferrer have helped bring attention to Afro-Cuban heritage. By recognizing these Latin Americans with direct African heritage, we honor all.

My Name Is Rocío

My grandparents were Spaniards. I live in Boston. I am Latina.

We reached the port of Alicante barefoot,
pushing Amaya and Arguiñe's baby carriage,
about to break.
Ricardo, waiting on the bridge of the ship,
let out a cry of relief:
"I thought you wouldn't make it!"
As the ship was leaving port with its cargo of refugees,
I looked at the desperate faces of those left behind,
with no other ships in sight.
I've often wondered at their fate—
since the next day
the sinister forces of the dictator Franco
took over Alicante.

    "Where did you find it?"
Abuelita asks, looking at the book I am reading.
"It was on the top shelf.
  Is this your diary, Abu Amaya?"
"That diary was written with tears.

My father wrote it for your mother and your uncles.
'Because they need to know,' he said. Now it's yours."
    I'm glad it's Saturday, because
I can't stop reading.
This is my great-grandfather's diary,
but it is also my story—
the story that explains why I was born in Boston
and also who I am.
It seems I've always known
some of the facts—
but they become so real
in his own voice.

My mother's family
left Spain because of the Spanish Civil War.
Abu Amaya was in that baby carriage
along with her brother.
She grew up in Mexico
and there married the son of other Spanish
immigrants.
So when my mother was born in Mexico,
she always knew she was also a Spaniard,
like her own parents—a child of the war.
My father's family
was also able to leave Spain,
although they left by walking—
up the high Pyrenees and into France.
They managed to reach Cuba,
and there my grandma grew up
and later my father also.
Mom and Dad say that when they met in college,
they immediately recognized that they were
two of a kind,
having grown up listening to the same stories.
Grandchildren of Spaniards
meeting in Boston, Massachusetts,
but always holding Spain in their hearts.

A year ago I went with Abu Amaya to see Guernica—
the town where she was born, in the Basque Country,
the town that inspired Picasso
to paint the horror of the war.

How surprising that in a small country
there can be so many landscapes, food,
music, and people, different in each of the regions:
Galicia, Catalunya, the Basque Country, Castilla,
Andalucía.
It helped me understand
how my two grandmothers are so different.
Abuelita Lola is Andalusian, from the south of Spain,
the liveliest person I know.
She can sing all day long and say the funniest things.
My Abu Amaya is kind, but stern and rather silent.
Yet when they begin telling stories of back then,
they could be the same person.
Abuelita Lola gets serious,
Abu Amaya gets animated,
and there is the same sadness
in both,
the same outrage
in both,
and in both the same pain
for a dream that was destroyed
and the lives that were lost
when something went wrong, so wrong.
But then they both look at me
and tell me that there is much, very much,
to learn about and appreciate about this new Spain,
reborn from its own ashes.
This new Spain, they both hope
I will grow to love and cherish as they do.

The Spanish Civil War:
A Struggle for Justice

Spain came out of the Spanish-American War exhausted, militarily and politically. It became a moment of reflection for Spain's intellectuals, writers, and artists, who suggested that the time had come to look not outside the Spanish frontiers but within—to ask themselves what the future of their nation should be, now that it was no longer an imperial power. This group of thinkers came from all over Spain. Miguel de Unamuno and Pío Baroja were Basque, Don Ramón del Valle-Inclán was from Galicia, Azorín was from Alicante, Antonio Machado from Andalucía. They helped renew a national interest in both art and reflection, to question and to dream, not of expanding abroad but of creating a more just society at home.

At the same time there was profound unrest among the people. Spain was ruled by a powerful but small class of wealthy people. Workers and peasants lived in poverty, with very little hope of bettering their conditions. Looking at the examples of the United States, France, and their own former colonies, many Spaniards decided to try to eliminate the monarchy and form a republic.

They were successful. The king left the country in 1931 and went to live in Portugal. Many political parties were formed, and democratic elections were held for president, city mayors, and congress.

But these were not easy times in Europe. At least two

other powerful nations were under Fascist dictatorships: Italy, under Mussolini, and Germany, under Hitler. The Spanish Republic had only been in power for a couple of years. The government had established public schools for all children, including the children of the workers and peasants. They had also supported the arts and workers' rights. But the wealthy people who had once held great power opposed a government that had the interests of the poor as its goal.

The landowning class supported the uprising of a general with the same Fascist ideas as Mussolini and Hitler. General Francisco Franco revolted with part of the army against the government. Militias of civilians were organized to defend the democratically elected republic.

Hitler and Mussolini lent their support to Franco, and Spain became the proving ground for new planes and weapons that would soon be used in World War II. But democratic countries such as Britain and the United States remained neutral, and the republic tried to defend itself with its militias. Men without the right weapons or uniforms, wearing canvas shoes, fought against well-organized armies. The death toll on both sides was enormous. About one million people died in a country of less than forty million.

Some people fled as soon as the war began. Others left after Franco won and established his dictatorship. Some were able to leave by ship. Other crossed the high Pyrenees Mountains into France. Many came across the Atlantic to Argentina, Mexico, Cuba, Puerto Rico, and the United States.

They were farmers and workers, intellectuals and teachers, professors and doctors. They brought with them the determination to live in freedom: to start anew, make a living, support a family, and uphold their ideas of social justice.

Most of the writers, poets, and artists who had supported the republic fled Spain. They tried to find support for the democratically elected government and denounced with their words and paintings what was happening in Spain. Some were not able to escape: poet and playwright Federico García Lorca was taken out of his house and shot, while poet Miguel Hernández died in prison.

Among the many intellectuals and artists that settled in the United States were the poets Pedro Salinas and Jorge Guillén. The cellist Pau Casals, the Nobel Prize–winning poet Juan Ramón Jiménez, and the translator Zenobia Camprubí, who was Jiménez's wife, all lived in exile in Puerto Rico.

Not all exiles were people. A famous exile was the painting *Guernica* by Pablo Picasso, which depicts the devastation created by the bombing of the town of Guernica, in the Basque Country in the north of Spain. This painting, one of the most important of the twentieth century, stayed in the United

States for decades. Picasso would not allow it to be exhibited in Spain during the repressive Franco dictatorship.

Guernica did not return to Spain until 1981, after democracy was restored. The painting was originally placed at the Museo del Prado, and can now be seen at the Museo Reina Sofía.

The people who emigrated because of the Spanish Civil War expected that Franco's dictatorship would be short-lived and that they would be able to return home quickly. That did not happen. Instead, they stayed away, enriching their new countries with their culture and experiences.

My Name Is Lili

I am Guatemalan. I am Chinese.
I live in Los Angeles.
I am Latina.

My Name Is Michiko

I am Peruvian. I am Japanese,
a sansei.
I live in Los Angeles.
I am Latina.

I'm used to the expressions
of surprise and wonder
the first time people hear me
speaking Spanish.
They often make comments like,
"For you Chinese people,
learning languages must be easy."

Sometimes I get tired of explaining
that while it's true
I'm Chinese,
it's also true I'm a Latina,
a Latin American, a Guatemalan.
It's nice when I don't have to explain.
That's what happened when I first met
Michiko,
who is now my best friend.
We were both new in school
and were placed in a Spanish bilingual class.
She looked at me,
I looked at her,
and we both smiled.

We both knew.
I knew that she has had to explain
many times
that although she is the granddaughter
of Japanese grandparents,
Spanish is her first language.
Just as I have had to explain
that I am both Chinese and Latina.
It was easy to become friends,
knowing something about each other already.
We are both proud of our rich history.
I am sorry I do not speak more Chinese,
and Michiko
is sorry she only speaks a little Japanese.
But we are beginning to learn
our grandparents' languages.
If people continue
to think of us
as Chinese and Japanese,
it will be fun to at least speak
our heritage language.
In our case,
being best friends,
we both decided to learn
Chinese and Japanese.
We already know that two languages
are much better than one—
so imagine knowing four!

I'm Michiko,
and I agree
with all Lili has said.
I like the pride I feel
being from Peru—
a country with such extraordinary
ancient cultures—
and I feel the same pride
knowing that my grandparents' culture
is equally ancient and rich.
But above all
I love talking to people,
listening to what they have to say,
trying to understand
how much people
can have inside.
That's why I will continue
to study languages,
so that one day
I can speak
and listen
around the world
and always feel at home
and among friends.

Chinese Presence in Latin America

While the number of immigrants from Asia to Latin America has not been as large as those who went to North America or western Europe, significant waves of immigrants from China, Japan, and Korea began arriving in South America in the eighteenth century. Some had working contracts to go to specific countries, but many were smuggled in deplorable conditions among the cargo of boats.

These Asian workers had fled their countries because of the lack of work, in search of better opportunities for themselves and their families. They were often falsely promised land to own, but in most cases what they found were conditions close to slavery.

From the mid-1840s large numbers of Chinese workers, primarily from Guangdong, a region devastated by war and famine, were brought to the American continent to work on plantations, in mining, and in railway construction. Their history is one of success through sacrifice: although the owners of the plantations, mines, and railroads grew rich off their labor, these immigrants scrimped and saved until they could open their own businesses—often restaurants, convenience stores, laundries, and vegetable stands.

By the mid-twentieth century, new waves of immigrants came from Taiwan, working mainly in factories in the big cities of Panama, Cuba, Paraguay, and Bolivia, often in the clothing industry. Some of these Chinese and Taiwanese immigrants or their children, already Spanish speakers, eventually moved to the United States and became part of the US Latino population.

Today China is a powerful presence in Latin America, lending billions to Brazil, building cars in Uruguay, buying copper from Chile, shipping buses to Cuba and clothes to Mexico. Its strength in the world is unquestionable.

Notable Latinos with Chinese ancestry include Wifredo Lam, a world-renowned painter born in Cuba, with Chinese and African ancestry; Franklin Chang-Díaz, a NASA astronaut with Chinese and Costa Rican ancestry; and Amelia Lau Carling, an author-illustrator of children's books now living and publishing in the United States, with Chinese and Guatemalan heritage.

Japanese Presence in Latin America

Japanese workers began emigrating to Latin America in the late nineteenth century, particularly to Brazil, Mexico, and Peru. The Japanese created solid communities, relying on each other for support, including lending money to each other. By marrying among themselves, they assured the survival of their culture. Although they worked hard for very low wages, over time they were able to purchase small plots of land and later consolidate them into large cooperatives. Today Brazilian Japanese are the biggest exporters of orange juice to the world.

Many Latin American Japanese returned to Japan in the 1980s as the Japanese economy soared, sending their earnings back to their families to improve their standard of living. Notable Latin Americans of Japanese descent include the Peruvian poet José Watanabe, the Bolivian poet Pedro Shimose, and the Brazilian model Juliana Imai.

One very difficult passage in the history of Japanese Latinos is the internment of people of Japanese ancestry living in the United States during World War II. The US government forcibly moved 110,000 Japanese American citizens and Japanese residents into internment camps for the war's duration. The United States also pressured Latin American nations to deport their Japanese, German, and Italian citizens to the United States to be interned in the camps. More than two thousand Japanese Latinos were interned in the camps, with eighty percent of those from Peru. They suffered the

indignity of being disowned by their own countries and deported to a foreign country with a language they did not speak. Because some of them only spoke Spanish, they were very isolated in the camps.

The postwar history of Japanese Latinos has not always been a happy one. The 1988 Civil Liberties Act allowed $20,000 in reparations to each Japanese American who had been interned, or to their heirs. Initially this reparation excluded Japanese Latinos. A later lawsuit assigned some reparation, but only $5,000 per person interned. Some Latin American Japanese who had been interned in the United States tried to return to Latin America, but they were not received; they had to go to Japan instead. But their children, born in Latin America, did not feel comfortable living in Japan, which led to many family conflicts.

Despite these difficulties, today descendants of Japanese immigrants continue to contribute to the development of Latin American societies.

My Name Is Andrés

I am both Colombian and Ecuadorian.
I live in Miami.
I am Latino.

The Mall of the Americas—
that's the favorite place for my relatives to visit
when they come to Miami from Colombia.
We separate into different groups.
Dad goes with Tío Julio.
They always return with lots of packages
and secret smiles—
no need to ask if they had fun.
I go with Ricky. He goes crazy
looking for music, gadgets, and games.
"It's not that we don't have it in Bogotá," he tells me,
"but it is cheaper here."
I wish I could go with Mom, though.
She takes Tía Rosario to special shops
to buy medical instruments
for her practice.

Tía sometimes buys two or three of the same thing.
"It's for my colleague in the clinic,
   Dr. San Juan. He's not fond of traveling," she says.
"With what we save, we can bring the kids to Florida,"
   I heard Tío Julio say.
   I know how much Isabel
   loves the Everglades.
   She wants to be a biologist,
   and already she plays the part,
   with her fatigues and net hat,
   her waterproof boots and her oversize
   backpack.

I must say that at first
I was afraid of her determination
to wait with a book at an outside café
until we were done with shopping.
When it was her time to choose,
nobody dared stop
this girl on her exploration
of the Florida Everglades.
I wanted to know why she found crocodiles and birds
so fascinating.
After asking her a thousand questions,
I wanted to go with her.
"Catastrophic!" she calls what is happening
in the Everglades. It's dying, she says,
and with it, the many species
that call this place home.
"But we can still save the Pantanal."
I had never heard of El Pantanal—
one of the biggest and richest
bio-environments on Earth,
extending into Brazil, Bolivia, and Paraguay.
"Extraordinary! A natural wonder!" she said,
and then she talked about
river otters and jaguars, toucans, tapirs, macaws,
anacondas and caimans, a hundred types of flowers,
and thousands of colored butterflies.
She convinced me.
Let's save the planet! *¡Ahora,* now, *ya!*

Latin America: Source of Biodiversity

Spreading from the Caribbean to Patagonia, Latin America is physically and topographically diverse. It is crossed by three of the largest rivers in the world—the Amazon, Orinoco, and Paraná—and by the Andes, the tallest mountain range in the Western Hemisphere. Striking glaciers coexist with desert sand dunes, and its rain forests are one the biggest natural reservoirs of plant and animal life on the planet. Some of the largest reservoirs of fresh water in the world are in the many large lakes in the Argentinian Patagonia.

The Amerindians, original inhabitants of this land, cultivated the land to support large populations and highly developed civilizations. They developed corn from a wild grass into an edible food source and cultivated many different kinds of potatoes, tomatoes, beans, and yucca.

Europeans who traveled to these lands brought back many products of the Americas. The significance of these contributions went well beyond enriching the European diet. Potatoes, in particular, prompted notable population growth in central Europe, since they could be left uncultivated underground throughout winter, safe from enemy armies.

Today, Latin American rain forests constitute a vital reserve of diverse plants and animals, many of whose benefits for humanity are yet to be discovered. The whole world must unite to preserve the unexplored reserves of the rich and diverse lands of Latin America.

My Name Is Román

I am Hispanic, *Hispano, Español,* Native American. I live in New Mexico. I am Latino.

My brother Lupe returned from jail
slimmer, sadder, silent, and solemn.
He said his bad days were over,
and with that, he sat at the door of our house
with a knife in one hand and a stick in the other.
Not a great recovery, I thought at first, but then I saw
saints coming out of those pieces of wood.
Saint Francis was his favorite. Saint Damien of
Molokai, the Child of Atocha, the Virgin of Guadalupe.
He sat there all summer, at the edge of the road,
in the town of Madrid, in the Turquoise Trail,
between Albuquerque and Santa Fe,
in the state of New Mexico.
By the time he stood up, he was an artist—
and a good salesman, too, as every tourist that drove by
stopped to see, and inevitably buy,

the precious *santos de palo* that he sculpted,
and sometimes also painted.
Lupe became famous.
He said art saved him.
I say he saved art.
Lupe saved the art of our native cultures
along the river Pecos.
A mix of Spanish and indigenous genius,
born from European fathers and native mothers,
all along the Southwest. And I,
who was destined to drop out at fourth grade,
became interested in what Lupe called OUR IDENTITY.
"Shame is the shadow of ignorance," he told me.

"It's okay if others ignore your history and your heritage.
But it is a crime if you do. Remember this, Román.
Never forget who you are."
One day he took me to see history
at the Museum of Folk Art in Santa Fe.
As soon as I set foot in that place,
I knew I was growing up.
I was surrounded by Nativities,
paper shepherds, plaster virgins,
tin crosses, tin toys.
I recognized the materials, the images.
I remembered the occasions
and the faces of joy on my people.
On the walls were red-pepper wreaths
and precious forms of clay art.
There were photographs of
Father Casimiro's church in Chimayo,
pinto horses built with piñones,
paintings of stucco houses,
luminarias trimming our pueblos,
north of Taos,
in the night.
Lupe sat with me at the library,
and we read about the artist María Antonia Montoya,
creator of black-on-black pottery,
and about Iris Nampeyo, of the Tewa people.
"Our art was born right here, two thousand years ago!"
Silence in New Mexico is blue.

It runs freely between the mesas
and red canyons, in the pine-studded mountain ranges.
"It is thanks to this silence that
there are so many artists in this land," Lupe tells me
while we drive on I-25 South to Albuquerque.
We have read about Frederico Vigil and his
Mundos de mestizaje: the Miracle Wall.
For the past nine years, this artist has been
painting a mural that covers four thousand square feet
inside the tower of the Hispanic Cultural Center.
Vigil says that this "is a tribute to Hispanic
connectedness,
to the global mix of cultures—Roman, Arab, African,
Jewish, Native American—that makes us who we are."
I think about his words.
And, looking at these walls inside the tower,
I realize the strength of my heritage,
the contradictions of our history,
the battles won and lost
within our hearts.
We have been mixing for centuries.
Mixing our blood, and our faiths.
Mixing traditions, music, and dance.
Mixing our languages, our literatures.
Mixing us into a greater reality,
a larger identity.
One that is now called Latino.
Yes! We are Latinos.

Contributions of the Evolving Latino Culture

Latinos or Hispanics have lived in the territories now known as the United States for more than four centuries. Saint Augustine, Florida, was founded by Spaniards in 1565— more than two hundred years before the Declaration of Independence was signed in 1776. And two hundred seventy years before that, in 1506, Puerto Rico already had a Spanish population. In New Mexico, Texas, and Arizona, Spanish settlements were established in 1598, and new ones developed for almost a century until 1692. Although the border between the United States and Mexico has changed over time, the Southwest has been inhabited by people of Spanish descent continuously for hundreds of years.

Of the more than three hundred million people living in the United States, more than fifty million are Latinos. Of these, sixty-four percent are of Mexican descent. Other Latinos have their roots in the Caribbean, or in Central or South America. Many families have been in the United States for many generations.

Like most immigrants to the United States, Latinos become fluent English speakers by the second generation. But many Latinos recognize the value of their heritage language and maintain both languages.

The entrepreneurial spirit of Latinos, along with their creativity, skills, and work ethic have made them important contributors to the economic success of this country. There are more than three million Hispanic-owned businesses in the US, and this number is expected to double in the next decade.

The artistic and literary heritage of Latinos includes hundreds of exemplary writers, including Nobel Prize winners Gabriela Mistral and Pablo Neruda from Chile and Octavio Paz from Mexico. The early twentieth century brought unsurpassed artistic expression in Mexico: great muralists such as Diego Rivera and José Clemente Orozco expressed the struggles and hopes of their people, while painter Frida Kahlo experimented with form and color to explore her inner life. This rainbow of talent, creativity, and imagination has inspired a new generation of Latino writers and artists living in the United States.

Latinos embody an emerging identity, uniting descendants from Spain and from twenty-one countries in Latin America. We invite you to explore, recognize, and celebrate this culture, which has a vibrant presence in the United States. We trust that in doing so, you will find an inspiration to leave your own mark on history.

Acknowledgments

None of these vignettes has been based on a single individual. They are fictional compositions. We do want to acknowledge and thank our students, and the many hundreds of teachers, parents, and children who through the years have given us insights into their lives as Latinos.

While they will be too numerous to mention here—and acknowledging that we may be making omissions, we would like to thank in particular the following friends, who have enriched our lives with their presence and have taught us much through their reflections:

On being Mexican in the United States
Felipe Dávalos, Antonia López, Emerita Orta Camilleri, Elvira Amas, Rosalía Salinas, George Ancona, Oralia Garza de Cortés, and Marcos Guerrero

On being Cuban in the United States
Along with Alma Flor's large extended family: Silvia Dorta-Duque de Reyes, Lourdes Rovira, Toni de Miranda, Mari Nieves Díaz Méndez, and Tania Álvarez

On being Puerto Rican

Tony Baez, Gladys Cruz, Ricardo Fernández, Antonio Martorell, Nicholasa Mohr, and Eduardo Seda Bonilla

On being Dominican in the United States

Dulce María Pérez, Amalia, and the writings of Julia Alvarez

On being Sephardic in the United States

Sultana, who allowed Alma Flor to be with her during her last months on earth and shared her life; Raquel Benatar, Itzhak Emmanuel, and Sam Laredo

On being Zapotec in the United States

The students of the Stockton School District; the people of Teotitlán del Valle, who offered us extraordinary hospitality; sensitive educators from the doctoral program at the School of Education, University of San Francisco, who have worked for many years with the students in Teotitlán and have recorded their words and experiences: Nancy Jean Smith, James Ryan, Marcos Guerrero, Silvia Dorta-Duque de Reyes, and Lorena García

On the farmworkers' life and experiences

María Álvarez, Alfonso Anaya, Rosie Arenas, Ricardo Balderas, Frank Espinoza, Rosa Hernández, Marta López, Rosario Morales, Francisco Reveles, and Isidro Tarango; the *familias* of Pájaro Valley, California, and in particular Aracelli y Patti Casillas, María Eugenia Domínguez, and Enrique Gómez

On being Salvadorean in the United States
Vicky Flores and her family; René Colato

On being Panamanian in the United States
Bernice Randall and Santiago Wood

On being Spanish in the United States
Ana Cerro, Teresa Guillén, Solita Salinas, and Paqui Lillo

On being Latin American and Asian
Amelia Lau Carling and Junko Yokota

On being Latinos of mixed heritage
Rosalma, Alfonso, Miguel, and Gabriel Zubizarreta, Virgilú de Miranda Roure, Virginia Marie, Lauren, Allison, and Julia Roure

On being Latina or Latino
Suni Paz, Margie Berta Avila, and hundreds of friends, sisters, and brothers in this journey of discovering, cherishing, maintaining, and sharing our identity

Bibliography for Teachers and Parents

Afro-Latin@ Forum. http://www.afrolatinoforum.org/

Anzaldúa, Gloria. *Borderlands/La Frontera: The New Mestiza.* San Francisco: Spinsters/Aunt Lute, 1987.
———. *This Bridge We Call Home: Radical Visions for Transformation.* New York: Routledge, 2002.

Castro, Américo. *The Spaniards: An Introduction to Their History.* Berkeley, CA: University of California Press, 1971.

Cuba Cuban.com: About Cuba. http://www.cubacuban.com/info/index.shtml

Fuentes, Carlos. *The Buried Mirror: Reflections on Spain and the New World.* Boston: Houghton Mifflin, 1992.

Galeano, Eduardo. *Open Veins of Latin America: Five Centuries of the Pillage of a Continent. 25th Anniversary Edition.* New York: Monthly Review Press, 1997.
———. *Century of the Wind: Memory of Fire Trilogy.* Vol. 3. New York: W.W. Norton, 1998/2010.

Latino in America. http://www.cnn.com/SPECIALS/2009/latino.in.america/

Pew Hispanic Center, a project of the Pew Research Center. http://www.pewhispanic.org

Spain: Arts and Culture. http://www.spainculture.us/

The Spanish Civil War. http://www.donquijote.org/culture/spain/history/civilwar.asp

Weiner, Rebecca. "Sephardim" Jewish Virtual Library. http://www.jewishvirtuallibrary.org/jsource/Judaism/Sephardim.html

Additional Resources for Young People

Picture books

Alarcón, Francisco X. *Angels Ride Bikes and Other Fall Poems. Los ángeles andan en bicicleta y otros poemas de otoño.* New York: Children's Book Press, 1999.

Ancona, George. *Mi barrio/My Neighborhood (We Are Latinos).* New York: Children's Press, 2004.

Anzaldúa, Gloria and Consuelo Méndez. *Friends from the Other Side / Amigos del otro lado.* San Francisco: Children's Book Press, 1993.

Brown, Monica. 2005. *My Name Is Gabito. The Life of Gabriel García Márquez.* Flagstaff, AZ: Luna Rising, 2005.

Carling, Amelia Lau. *Mamá y Papá Have a Store.* New York: Dial Books, 1998.

Colato Laínez, René. *From North to South.* New York: Children's Book Press, 2010.

González, Lucía. *The Storyteller's Candle.* New York: Children's Book Press, 2008.

Middle-grade books

Ada, Alma Flor and Gabriel M. Zubizarreta. *Dancing Home.* New York: Atheneum, 2011.
——. *Love, Amalia.* New York: Simon and Schuster, 2012.

Alvarez, Julia. *Return to Sender.* Knopf, 2009.

Anaya, Rudolfo. *Elegy on the Death of César Chávez.* El Paso, Texas: Cinco Puntos Press, 2000.

Anderson, Joan. *Spanish Pioneers of the Southwest.* New York: Dutton, 1989.

Campoy, F. Isabel and Alma Flor Ada. *Tales Our Abuelitas Told.* New York: Atheneum, 2006.

Muñoz Ryan, Pam. *Esperanza Rising.* New York: Scholastic, 2000.
⸺. *Becoming Naomi León.* New York: Scholastic, 2004.
⸺. *The Dreamer.* New York: Scholastic, 2010.

Young adult books

Alvarez, Julia. *Before We Were Free.* New York: Knopf, 2002.

Bernier-Grand, Carmen. *Frida. ¡Viva la vida! Long Live Life!* New York: Marshall Cavendish, 2007.

Engle, Margarita. *The Surrender Tree. Poems of Cuba's Struggle for Freedom.* New York: Henry Holt, 2008.

Jiménez, Francisco. *The Circuit: Stories from the Life of a Migrant Child.* Albuquerque, NM: University of New Mexico Press, 1997.
⸺. *Breaking Through.* Boston: Houghton Mifflin, 2002.
⸺. *Reaching Out.* Boston: Houghton Mifflin, 2009.

McCall, Guadalupe García. *Under the Mesquite.* New York: Lee and Low, 2011.

Mohr, Nicholasa. *In My Own Words: Growing Up Inside the Sanctuary of My Imagination.* New York: Simon and Schuster, 1994.

Index